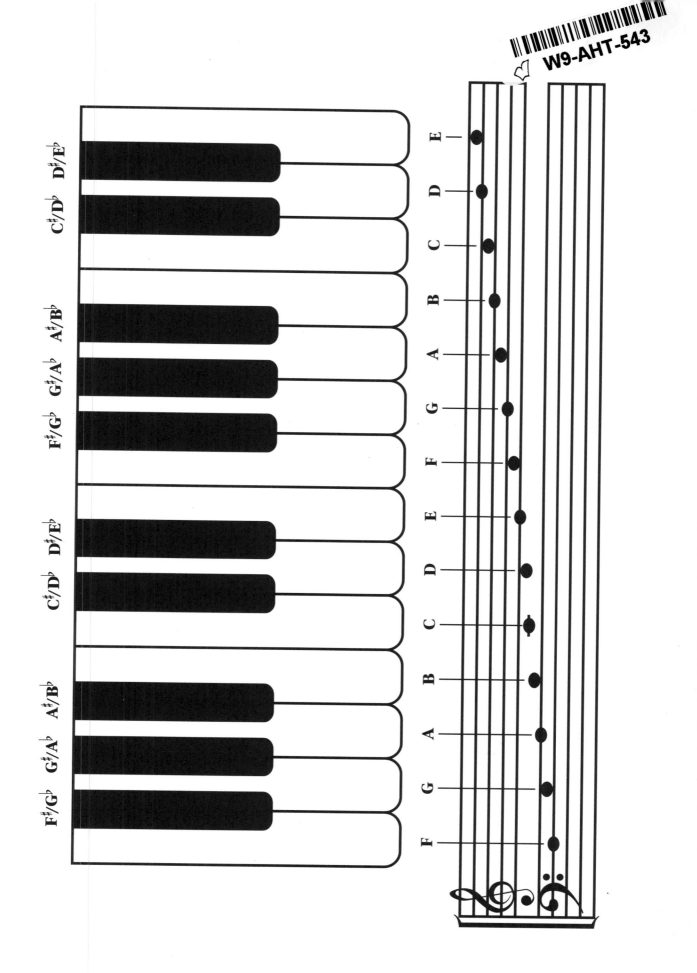

Silver Burdett MAKING MUSIC

Program Authors

Jane Beethoven
Susan Brumfield
Patricia Shehan Campbell
David N. Connors
Robert A. Duke
Judith A. Jellison

Rita Klinger
Rochelle Mann
Hunter C. March
Nan L. McDonald
Marvelene C. Moore
Mary Palmer
Konnie Saliba

Recording Producers

Rick Baitz
Rick Bassett
Joseph Joubert
Bryan Louiselle

Tom Moore
J. Douglas Pummill
Michael Rafter
Buryl Red, EXECUTIVE PRODUCER

Buddy Skipper
Robert Spivak
Jeanine Tesori
Linda Twine

Scott Foresman

Editorial Offices: Parsippany, New Jersey • Glenview, Illinois • New York, New York
Sales Offices: Parsippany, New Jersey • Duluth, Georgia • Glenview, Illinois
Coppell, Texas • Ontario, California

NOV 6 2002   ISBN: 0-382-34345-X

Contents

Steps to Making Music

Paths to Making Music

On the Move with Loud and Soft

How can you move to loud music?

How can you move to soft music?

Sing and **move** to the music.

1–4

A Different Beat

Words and Music by Bryan Louiselle

Keep It Steady

Steady beat is like your heartbeat.

Which things make a steady beat sound?

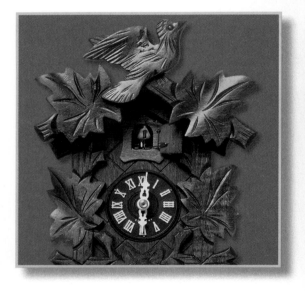

Windshield Wipers (Poem)

by Mary Ann Hoberman

Windshield Wipers

by Mary Ann Hoberman

Windshield wipers wipe the windshield

Wipe the water off the pane

This way	That way
This way	That way
This way	That way

In the rain.

Which music has a steady beat?

Watermelon Man

(excerpt) by Herbie Hancock

Silver Apples of the Moon

(excerpt) by Morton Subotnick

Birthday Rhythms!

Tap the steady beat.

1–16

Apples, Peaches, Pears, and Plums

Traditional Game Chant

Ap-ples, peach-es, pears and plums.

Tell me when your birth-day comes.

Rhythm is the pattern of the words.

Clap the rhythm of the words.

Ap-ples, peach-es, pears and plums.

Tell me when your birth-day comes.

Melody

High and Low

1–24

The Little Green Frog
Traditional Song from the United States

Listen to the song.

When does the **melody** leap high?

lump!

Ga-

Move like the little green frog.

Frogs like to leap in lily ponds!

Arts Connection

▲ *White Water Lilies* by Claude Monet (1840–1926)

Listen for high and low sounds.

1–25

Andante quieto

from *Three Nocturnes for Piano Trio* by Ernest Bloch

Phoebe Goes Up and Down

Sing the song "Phoebe."

Follow the direction of the melody.

Which lines of the song are the same?

Which lines of the song are different?

To TOWN

Phoebe

Folk Song from North Carolina

1–31

Phoe - be in her pet - ti - coat,

Phoe - be in her gown,

Phoe - be in her pet - ti - coat,

Go - ing down to town.

My Voice

We can use our voices in different ways.

How are the children using their voices?

1–35

Sing! Speak! Whisper! Shout!

Words and Music by Rick Bassett

Sing!

Speak!

Whisper!

Shout!

13

Expression

Fast or Slow?

1–51

Freight Train
Words and Music by E. Cotton

What can move **fast?**

What can move **slow?**

How can you **move** fast?

How can you **move** slow?

Rhythm

Rainy Day Rhythm

Sing the song.

Tap each umbrella on the steady beat.

Clap the rhythm of the words.

Rain,   rain,   go   a -   way,

Come a - gain some oth - er   day.

Read the rhythm.

2–12

Rain, Rain
Traditional Children's Song

Rain,   rain,   go   a - way.

Come   a - gain   some   oth - er   day.

Answer the Call

When someone calls, you answer.

Pat on the **call.**

Clap on the **response.**

call

response

2-14

Shortnin' Bread
African American Folk Song

Create your own response.

19

Melody

Sailing High and Low

Charlie's boat sails up and down.

Sing the song and follow his boat.

Point to each boat on the beat.

The melody goes high and low.

What Makes That Sound?

What do you see in the pictures?

Listen to the sounds.

What makes each sound?

2–28
Junk Music Montage

I can make sounds, too!

Clap, Tap, and Pat

People create music in different ways.

People sing and play instruments.

People clap, tap, pat, and stamp.

▲ Maori *poi* ball dancers

To'ia mai te waka

Maori Folk Song from New Zealand

Move on the steady beat of the song.

Paddle the canoe.

M·U·S·I·C M·A·K·E·R·S

Kiri Te Kanawa

Kiri Te Kanawa is a famous singer.
She is from New Zealand.

2–33

Piki mai

**Maori Welcome Song
from New Zealand**

25

Soft Pops Loud Pops

2–43

We're Making Popcorn
by Judith Thomas

Old-fashioned popcorn was made in a pan.

Pop **Pop**

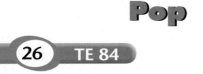

When is the sound soft?

When is it the loudest?

Pop Pop Popcorn

Planting Long and Short Sounds

Rice is grown all over the world.

People grow rice in many different ways.

2-47

Cha yang wu (Rice Planting Song)

Folk Song from China

Sing the song.

Read and **clap** this rhythm pattern.

Hai hai   huh,   hai hai   ho,

Plant-ing   rice is   ver-y   nice.

Moving

Soccer Sounds and Silences

Pretend you are a soccer player.

Listen to the music.

Dribble the ball and **move** on the beat.

Stop the ball on the silent beat.

3–1

¡Viva el fútbol!
(I Love Soccer)

Words and Music by Moretto and Bassett

Soc-cer   is my   game.

It's the   best by   far.

Same or Different?

The Rain Sings a Song

Words and Music by Irving Lowens

Sing a song about rain.

What parts of the song are the same?

What parts are different?

Play this pattern as you sing.

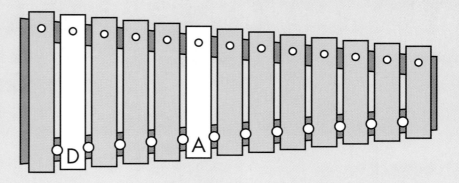

Create an accompaniment for the song.

Meet so and mi

3–15

Star Light, Star Bright
Traditional Song from the United States

Sing and point to the stars.

High and low sounds have musical names.

Read *so* and *mi* on the staff.

so

so   mi   so   mi

▲ *Starry Night* (1889)
by Vincent van Gogh

so

mi

Thump, Rattle, and Scrape

Listen to these instruments.

How is each one played?

Tabla ▶

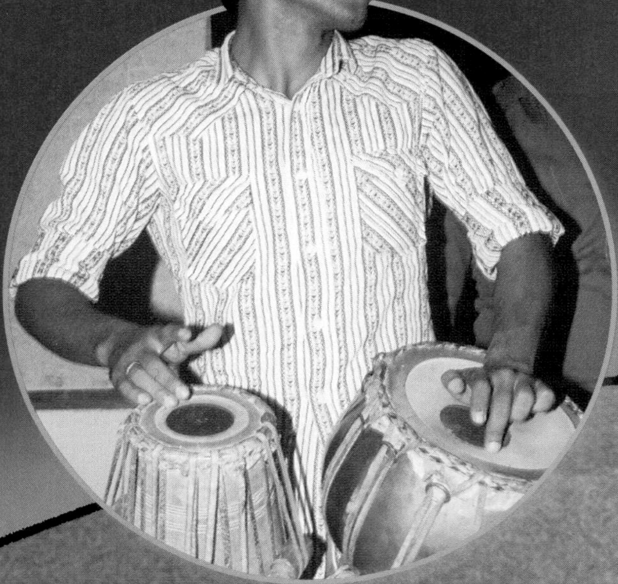

Shekere
▼

Djembe ▲

Taiko drums ▼

▲ **Timpani**

Snare ▲
drum

◄ *Guiro, maracas,*
and claves

37

Faster, Faster, Stop!

Change the **tempo** as you say the poem.

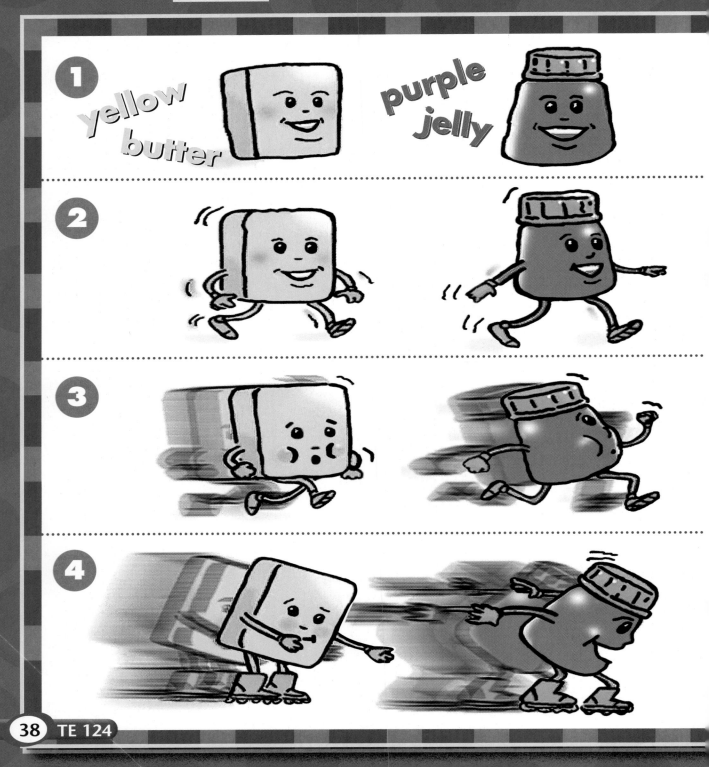

1 yellow butter   purple jelly

2

3

4

Cat at Rest

A **rest** is a beat with no sound.

Read and **clap** the rhythms.

Form

Verse and Refrain

This song has two sections.

It has a **verse** and a **refrain**.

4–2

Nampaya omame
(There Come Our Mothers)
Traditional Zulu Song from South Africa

Rock forward and back on the verse.

Rock from side to side on the refrain.

Form

Two Different Sections

This song has two different sections.

Call the first section **A**.

Call the second section **B**.

4–9

Amefuri (Japanese Rain Song)
School Song from Japan

Play the steady beat on a  in section A.

A

Play the rhythm on ♩ in section B.
Make the ♩ sound like gentle rain.

B

Melody

Bounce to a New Note

Balls can bounce high and low.

A melody can go high and low.

Bounce High, Bounce Low

Traditional Game Song from the United States

Listen for the *so* and *mi* pitch patterns in this song.

| so | ? | so | mi |

| so so | ? ? | so | mi |

The new pitch is *la*.

so | so | la | so | mi

so so | la la | so | mi

Timbre

4–22

Chang
(Elephant)
Folk Song from Thailand

Instrument Sounds

Music is a part of celebrations everywhere.

In Thailand there is a celebration for elephants.

Listen to this song about elephants.

These instruments are from Thailand.

How are they played?

49

UNIT 5

Expression

Getting Louder, Getting Softer

Listen! A band is far away.

Clap the beat.

The Parade Came Marching

Words and Music by John Forster

Listen for the loud and soft

parts in this famous march.

The Stars and Stripes Forever

by John Philip Sousa

Beats in Two

Beats can be grouped in sets of two.

The first beat is the strong beat.

Play your cymbals on the strong beat.

| Knock the | cym-bals, | do, oh, | do, |

| Knock the | cym-bals, | do, oh, | do, |

Knock the Cymbals
Play-Party Game from Texas

This song is written in meter in two.

2/4

Knock the cym - bals, do, oh, do,

Knock the cym - bals, do, oh, do,

Knock the cym - bals, do, oh, do,

Hel - lo, Su - san Brown - o.

Form

A Dance in Two Parts

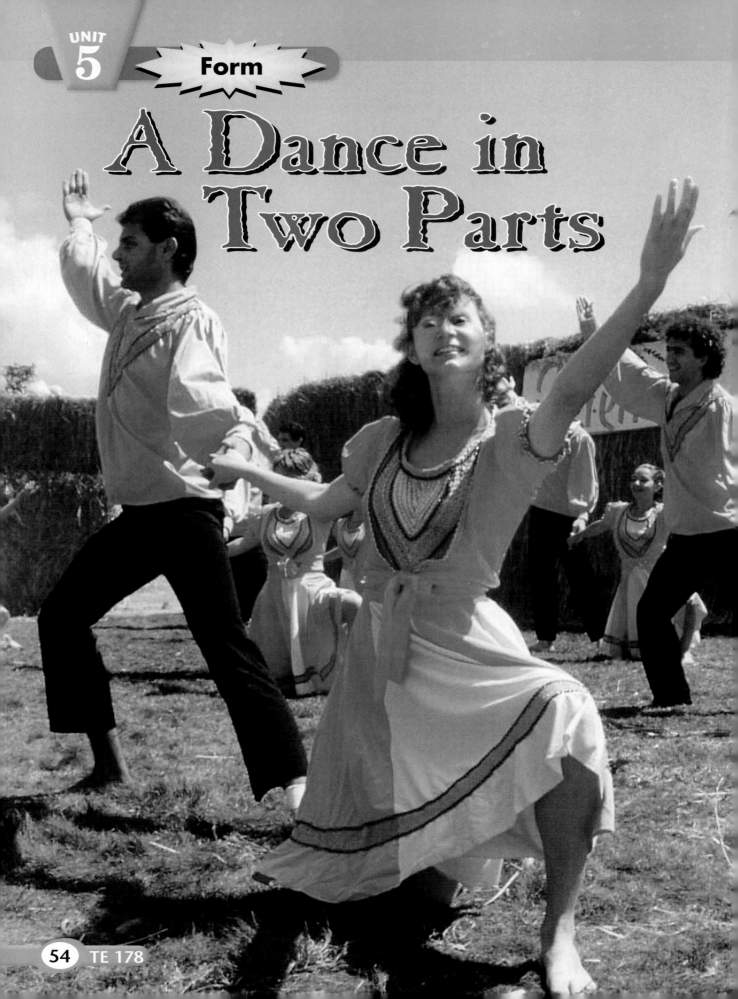

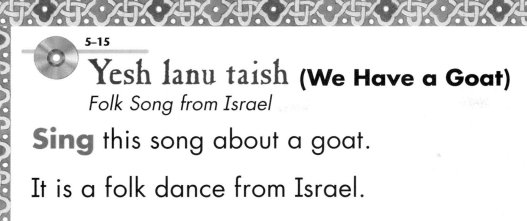

Yesh lanu taish (We Have a Goat)

Folk Song from Israel

Sing this song about a goat.

It is a folk dance from Israel.

How will you **move** on the verse?

How will you **move** on the refrain?

More *so*, *mi*, and *la*

5-29

Snail, Snail
Traditional Children's Song

Follow the snails.

Read the pitches.

so | 2/4

so   mi   so   mi

so so la la so so mi

Lemonade
Children's Game Song

so **2/4** Here we come.

Where from?

New York.

What's your trade?

Lem - on - ade.

Give us some, don't be a - fraid.

Timbre

Ding! Dong! Bong!

Musical instruments have their own special sounds.

Listen to these instruments.

5-37

Hard Times
by Len "Boogsie" Sharpe

Where might you hear
this instrument being played? ▶

5-38

Sekar jepun

**Traditional Balinese Kebyar
Gamelan Music**

Fast or Slow? Loud or Soft?

6–9
Hungarian Dance No. 3
by **Johannes Brahms**

Listen for three sections in this music.

1

Marin Alsop

Conductors lead orchestras, bands, and choirs.

Marin Alsop is the conductor of the Colorado Symphony Orchestra.

She directs the musicians when to play loud or soft, fast or slow.

How is each one different?

2

3

Rug Bug Rhythms

6–16

Little Black Bug

Words by Margaret Wise Brown
Music by Ruth Boshkoff

Read the rhythm patterns.

Play them on a 🥁 or a △.

Lit - tle   black   bug,

Bug,   ugh,   ugh.

Create your own patterns using

♩ , ♫ , and 𝄽 .

Arts **Connection**

Cuna Indian Molas from
the San Blas Islands ▶

Moving

Same Different Same

6–22

B-A, Bay

Folk Song from the United States

Listen for the different sections in this song.

How many sections do you hear?

A

Pat and **clap** in section **A**.

Move to show the different sections.

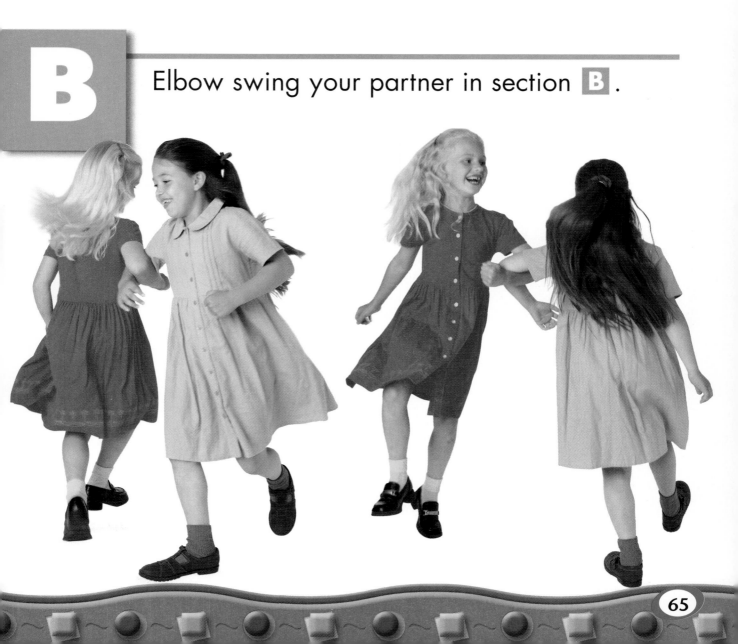

Elbow swing your partner in section B.

Look Out Below, Here Comes do!

Sing the song "Apple Tree."

Use pitch names *so*, *mi*, and *la*.

Apple Tree

Traditional Song from the United States

6–29

do

Ap - ple tree, ap - ple tree,

Will your ap - ples fall on me?

I won't cry and I won't shout,

If your ap - ple knocks me out.

Hum the new note.

Is it higher or lower than *so*?

Is it higher or lower than *mi*?

The new note is called *do*.

do

Xylobone or Xylophone?

Create an accompaniment for this poem about fossils.

Play your accompaniment on a .

6–32

🔘 **Mammoth (poem)**

by **Richard Edwards**

Mammoth

(excerpt)

by *Richard Edwards*

Once I waved my wild tusks high,

Once I was colossal,

Now I never see the sky,

Now I'm just a fossil.

Some musical instruments are made of wood.

Listen for the xylophone in this music.

What other instruments do you hear?

6–33

Fossils

from *Carnival of the Animals*
by Camille Saint-Saëns

Fossils Listening Map

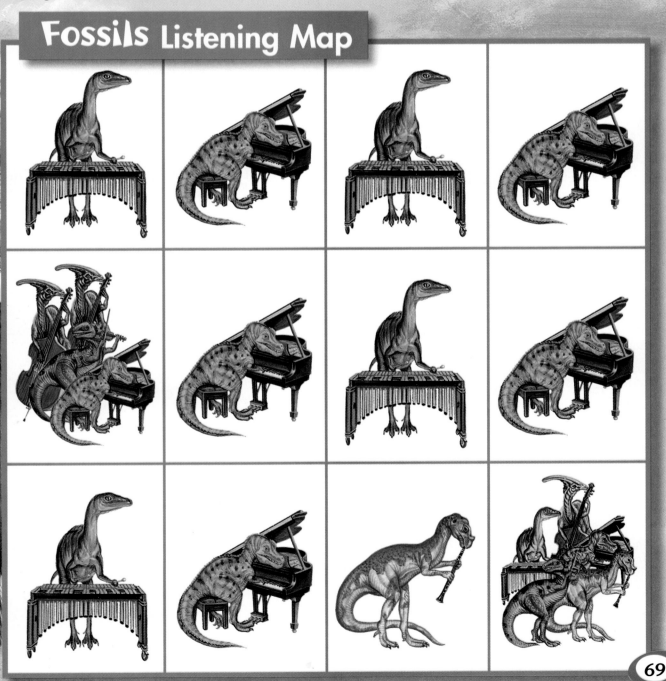

Moving

Ant Antics

7-4
The Ants Go Marching

Words Adapted by Edith Fowke
Music by Patrick S. Gilmore

1 one

2 two

3 three

4 four

5 five

6 six

We sing counting songs at school.

Pat the steady beat.

Meet the Instruments

7–14
The Little Red Hen
by Judith Thomas

Bok bok bok bok bok bok bok-ee!

Listen to the story of the Little Red Hen.

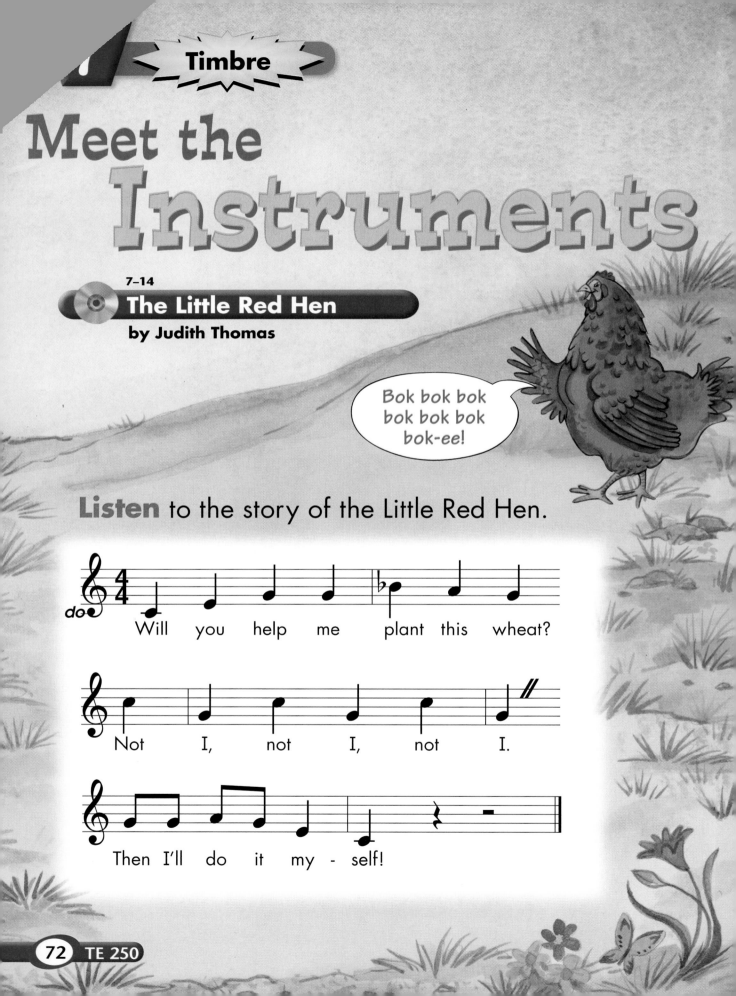

Will you help me plant this wheat?

Not I, not I, not I.

Then I'll do it my - self!

Someday you might play in a school orchestra.

Here are some instruments you might play.

Listen for the special sound of each instrument.

The Little Red Hen Listening Map

Moving

Sing and Spell

Sing this song and spell the words.
What other words can you spell?

___og

___an

___op

___c at

7–30

I Can't Spell Hippopotamus

Words and Music by J. Fred Coots

· ·

hat   **cat**   **fat**

· ·

dog   **log**   **hog**

· ·

top   **hop**   **mop**

· ·

ban   **man**   **fan**

We Sing About Our Country

Sing a song about America.

Listen for words that name places.

7–32

This Land Is Your Land

(Refrain only)
Words and Music by Woody Guthrie

This land is your land,

This land is my land,

From California to the New York Island;

From the redwood forest

To the Gulf Stream waters;

This land was made for you and me.

7–34

You're a Grand Old Flag

by George M. Cohan

Moving

A Bump-a-Deedle Dance

How do you do the Bump-a-Deedle dance?

How many ways can you **move?**

Create your own Bump-a-Deedle dance.

8–11

Everybody Says

Words and Music by Malvina Reynolds

Ev - ery - bo - dy bump a dee - dle dance with me.

Alvin Ailey

American Dance Theater

These dancers perform all over the world.
They move to different kinds of music.
They create many shapes with their bodies.

My Family and Me

Families Work and Sing Together

This family lives in Peru.

How can families work together?

8–16

Los maizales

(The Cornfields)

Folk Song from Peru

Music can have layers of sound.

Listen to this music from Peru.

What instruments do you hear?

Tema de maimara **Listening Map**

8–15

Tema de maimara
Traditional Andean

81

Singing in the Tub

Bath time can be fun.

Some people sing in the bath.

Sing this bath time song.

Follow the pictures.

8–24

Scrub-a-Dub

Words and Music by David Eddleman

Glub-a glub!

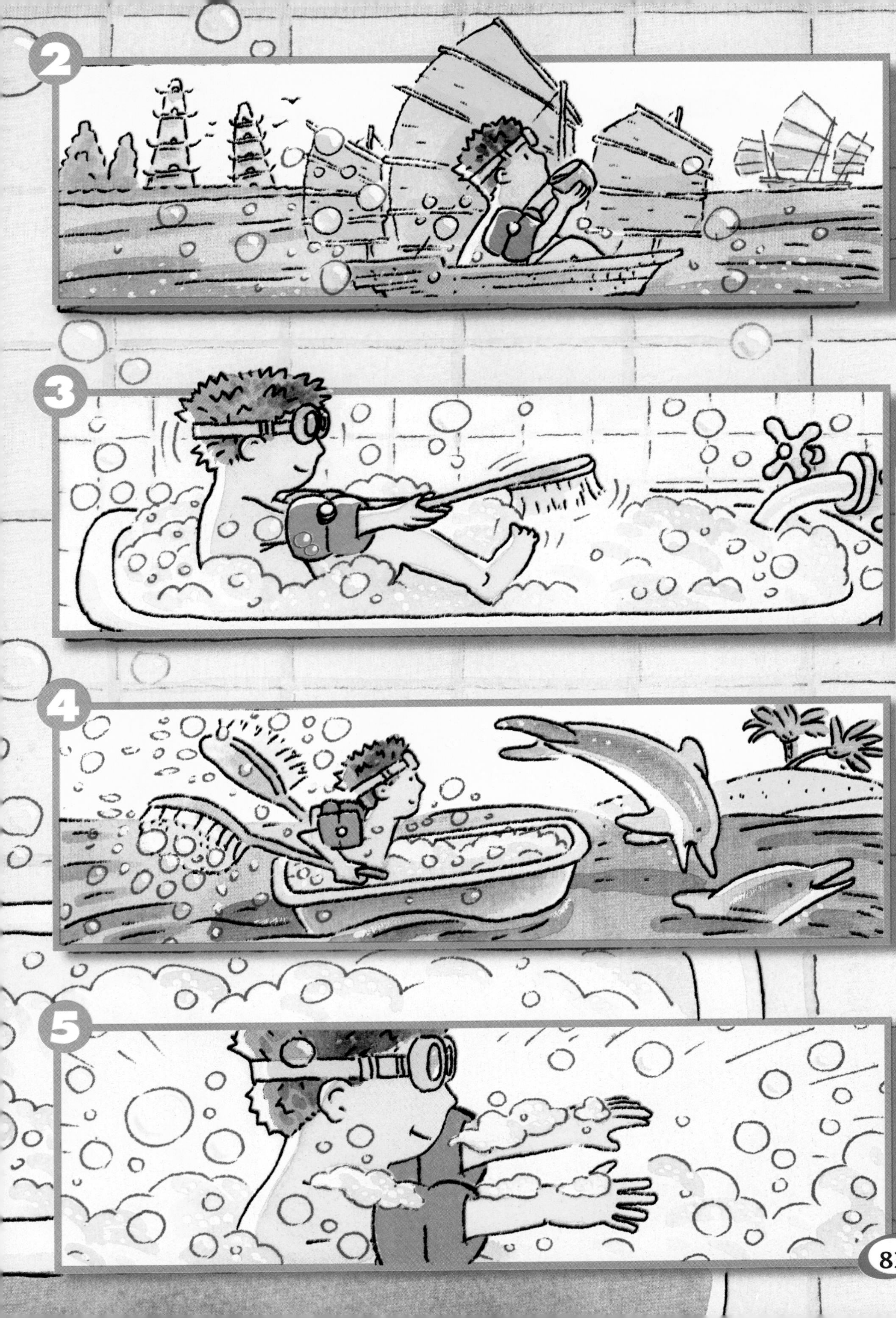
2
3
4
5

Families Around the World

You are an important member of a family.

How are families alike?

How are they different?

Sing this song about families.

Play this rhythm pattern on 🥁 or a △.

8–31
Families
Words and Music
by James A. Forbes, Jr.

Singing

How Do You Sing Hello?

People say *hello* in many ways.

Sorida

Game Song from the Shona People of Zimbabwe

Sing and **move** to *"Sorida."*

How can you say *hello* without using words?

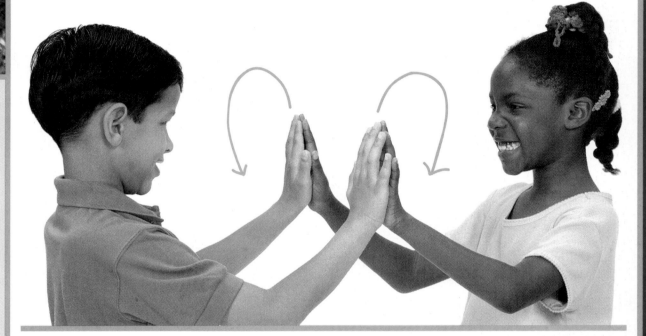

Moving

musical GAMES

Sing and say this jump rope rhyme.

Pat and **clap** the steady beat.

9–2

Banana Splits
Jump-rope Rhyme

Banana, banana, banana splits,
Mama had a baby chick.
Chick was a hen,
Do it over again,
Banana, banana, banana splits.

Green, Green, Rocky
African American Singing Game

9–4

Listen to "Green, Green, Rocky."

Find this pattern in the song.

do — Rock - y

Adventures with Friends

89

Friends Make Music

What is a friend?

This poem tells about being a friend.

How to Be a Friend
by Pat Lowery Collins

Keep a secret
Tell a wish
Listen
to
a dream

Create an ABA form.

The poem is the A section.

Create a B section using instruments.

Arts **Connection**

▶ *Patticake* (1986)
by Brenda Joysmith

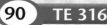

Listen for special sounds in the song.

Create sound effects to accompany the song.

Two by Two

Sing this song about animals.

How are the animals walking?

Play a walking sound on the drum.

9–24
Noah's Shanty

Words and Music by Malcolm Abbs

Play this accompaniment.

Sea Treasures

Say this speech piece.

Pat and **clap** the steady beat.

9–29

Beach Rap
by Judith Thomas

Going on a shell walk,
Grand sandy beach,
Looking for the treasures
That are in my reach!

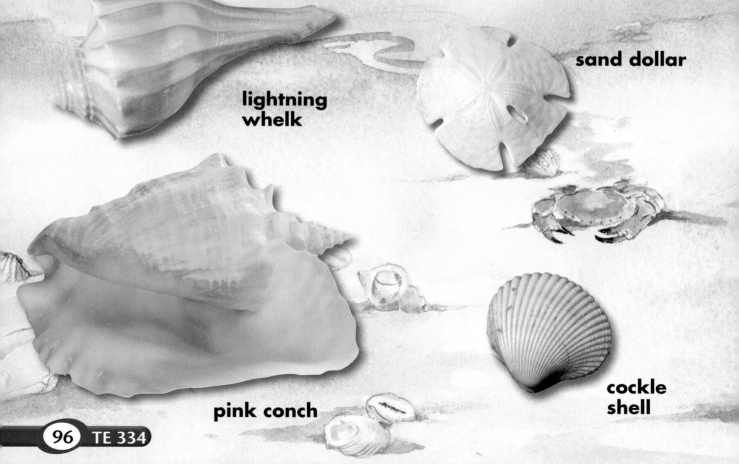

sand dollar

lightning
whelk

pink conch

cockle
shell

Create rhythm patterns with shell names.

Play the patterns on instruments.

purple
scallop

alphabet
cone

worm shell

baby's ear
moon

auger shell

A Flutter of Butterflies

Sing the song. Which parts are alike?

10–3

Ah! Les jolis papillons

(Ah! The Pretty Butterflies)

Folk Song from St. Pierre and Miquelon

Each winter, monarch butterflies fly to Mexico.

Arts Connection

▲*Untitled* (1997)
by Bob Marstall

Listen for the fluttering sounds of butterflies in this music.

10–7

Butterfly

by Edvard Grieg

A Spring Dance

Winters in Russia are long.

Russian people celebrate when spring comes.

They dance and sing songs about growing things.

10–19

Khorovod (Round Dance)
Folk Song from Russia

Follow the directions and **move** to the music.

A Song of Wishful Thinking

Where would you like to go?

What would you like to be?

Think about it as you **sing** this song.

10–25

Just Imagine

Words and Music by Philip A. Parker

Just imagine, just imagine
Just imagine all the things
that we could be,
Imagine all the places
we could go and see,
Imagination's fun for you and me.

What do you see?

103

Sing Me a Story

Sing this story song.

How does the story end?

10–34
I Know an Old Lady

Words by Rose Bonne
Music by Alan Mills

Listen to another version of the song.

How are the two versions different?

10–35
I Know an Old Woman

by Bonne and Mills
as performed by The King's Singers

Imagination Station!

105

Movin' On with a Silly Song

What do you think this song is about?

Sing this silly song.

11-1

Hi Heidi Ho

*Words and Music
by Lucille Panabaker*

Play these rhythm patterns.

Make up a funny walk.

Teach it to a friend.

Musical Journey to Jupiter

Let's take a musical trip to the planet Jupiter.

Jupiter is the largest planet in our solar system.

11–16

Jupiter

from *The Planets*
by Gustav Holst

Listen to this music about Jupiter.

What happens to the tempo?

What instruments do you hear?

M·U·S·I·C M·A·K·E·R·S

Gustav Holst

Gustav Holst (1874–1934) was a composer.
He loved to study about the stars and planets.
He wrote music about the planets.

Play a Birthday Pattern

Which pattern will you **play**?

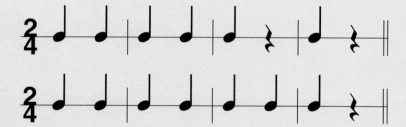

Which instrument will you use?

hand drum   tambourine   rhythm sticks

The End
by A. A. Milne

When I was One,
I had just begun.

When I was Two,
I was nearly new.

When I was Three,
I was hardly me.

When I was Four,
I was not much more.

When I was Five,
I was just alive,

But now I am Six, I'm clever as clever.
So I think I'll be Six for ever and ever.

11–20
The End (poem)
by A. A. Milne

Sing and Celebrate the Season

People celebrate holidays in different ways.

Singing and dancing are part of many celebrations.

A Patriotic Song

Sing this special song about our country.

Follow the direction of the melody.

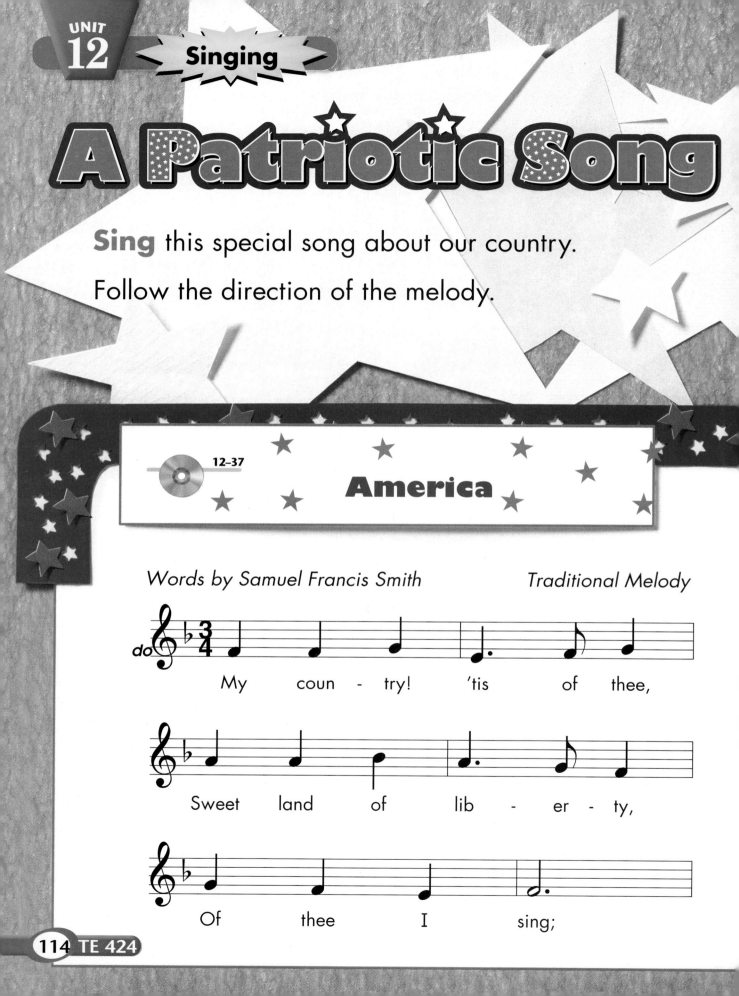

12–37

America

Words by Samuel Francis Smith

Traditional Melody

My coun - try! 'tis of thee,

Sweet land of lib - er - ty,

Of thee I sing;

Mallet Instruments

▲ Xylophone

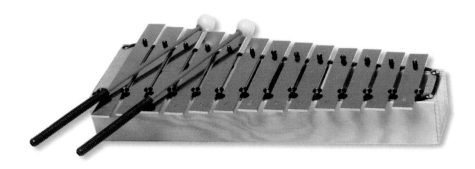

▲ Glockenspiel

Hold the mallets correctly.

Strike the bar in the center.

◀ Alto metallophone

Play this **bordun.**

Sound Bank

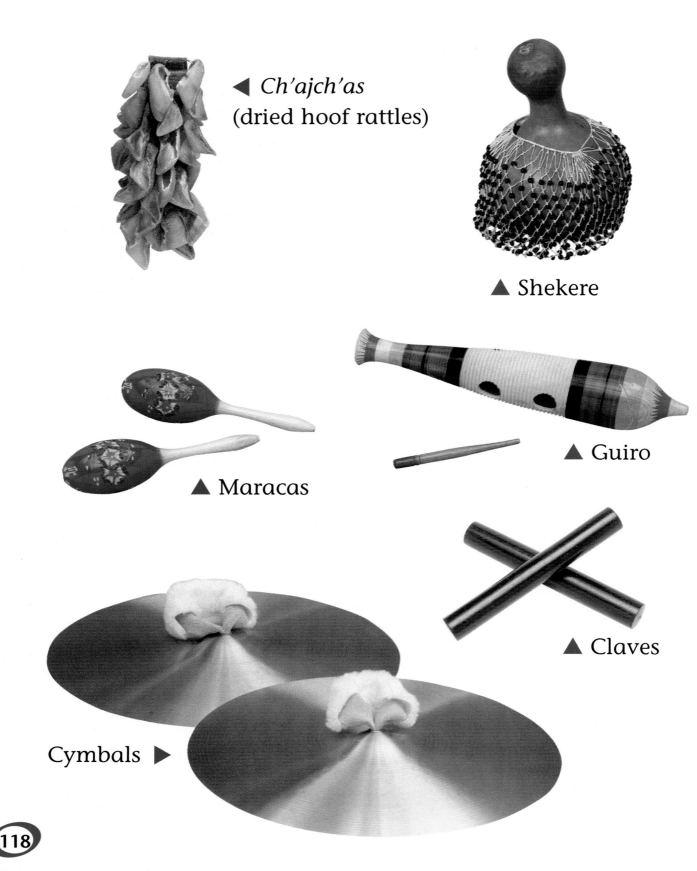

◀ *Ch'ajch'as*
(dried hoof rattles)

▲ Shekere

▲ Maracas

▲ Guiro

▲ Claves

Cymbals ▶

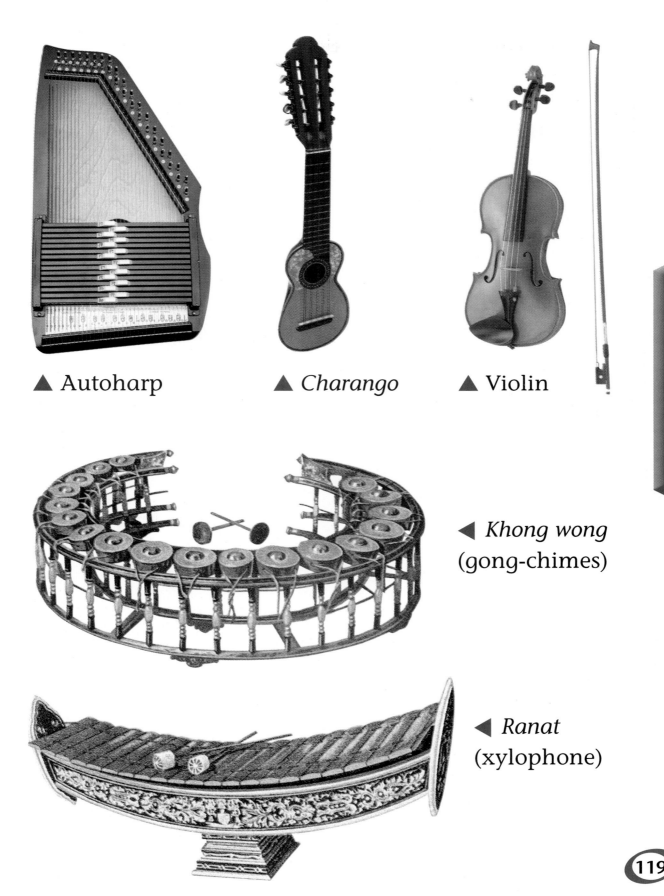

▲ Autoharp

▲ *Charango*

▲ Violin

◀ *Khong wong*
(gong-chimes)

◀ *Ranat*
(xylophone)

▲ *Bombo*

◀ *Tabla*

◀ *Timpani* ▶

Taiko drum ▶

▲ *Snare drum*

▲ *Djembe*

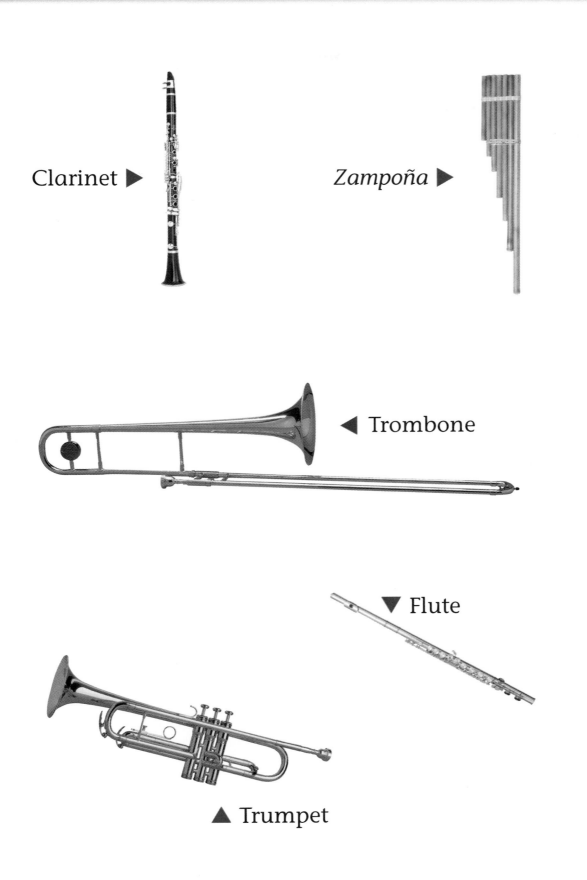

Clarinet ▶

Zampoña ▶

◀ Trombone

▼ Flute

▲ Trumpet

Index of Songs

and Speech Pieces

Credits

Cover Photography: Jade Albert for Scott Foresman
Cover Design: Steven Curtis Design, Inc.

Photograph Credits

4: (CR) © Myrleen Ferguson/PhotoEdit 4: (BR) © Nancy Sheehan/PhotoEdit 9: (TC) Scala/Art Resource, NY 14: (B) © Peter Weimann/Animals Animals/Earth Scenes 14: (C) Joe McDonald/Animals Animals/Earth Scenes 15: (CR) courtesy Arlington National Racecourse 15: (BL) © David Stoecklein/The Stock Market 15: (BR) ©J. & P. Wegner/Animals Animals/Earth Scenes 24: (B) SuperStock 24: (B) PhotoDisc 25: (B) Jack Vartoogian 28: (BC) ©S. Michael Bisceglie/Animals Animals/Earth Scenes 28: (CL) ©Grant Heilman/Grant Heilman Photography 28: (Bkgd) PhotoDisc 30: (BL) © Richard Hutchings/PhotoEdit 30: (CR) John Garrett/© Dorling Kindersley 30: (CR) John Garrett/© Dorling Kindersley 30: (BC) John Garrett/© Dorling Kindersley 32: (BC) SuperStock 32: (BR) © Richard Hutchings/PhotoEdit 35: (T) van GOGH, Vincent. "The Starry Night." (1889) Oil on canvas, 29 x 36 1/4" (73.7 x 92.1 cm). The Museum of Modern Art, New York. Acquired through the Lillie P. Bliss Bequest. Photograph ©2002 The/Museum of Modern Art, New York 36: (CL) Jack Vartoogian 36: (CR) Dirk R. Franz/Hutchison Library 36: (BR) © Crispin Hughes 36: Owen Franken/Corbis 37: (TL) Milt & Joan Mann/Cameramann International, Ltd. 37: (CR) © James McCormick 37: Marilyn Rife Warren Johnson/Marilyn Rife 37: (T) Tony Freeman/PhotoEdit 40: (B) Staatl. Galerie Moritzburg, Halle/A.K.G., Berlin/SuperStock 42: (C) Milt & Joan Mann/Cameramann International, Ltd. 48: Dave G. Houser (C) Jan Butchofsky-Houser 49: Jack Vartoogian 52: © Dorling Kindersley 53: Corbis 53: (T) © Dorling Kindersley 54: (C) ASAP 58: (B) © Pablo Corral/Corbis 58: (L) Photo © Barry Dawson, from Traditional Indonesian Textiles by John Gillow, published by Thames and Hudson Inc., New York 59: (BL) © George Holton/Photo Researchers, Inc. 60: (TC) Jim Zuckerman/Corbis 61: (C) Colorado Symphony Association 62: Kevin Schafer 63: Kevin Schafer 73: Artville 76: (CL) PhotoDisc 76: (BL) PhotoDisc 76: (CR) Rohan/Stone 76: (BR) © Maresa Pryor/Animals Animals/Earth Scenes 78: (Bkgd) TH-Foto Werbung/Art Directors & TRIP Photo Library 79: (B) © Hulton-Deutsch Collection/Corbis 84: (B) ©97 Ronnie Kaufman/The Stock Market 84: Wolfgang Kaehler/Corbis 85: (TR) ©Dwayne Newton/PhotoEdit 85: (BL) ©Sotographs/Liaison Agency 85: (TL) © P. DeWilde/Liaison Agency 85: (BR) ©Stewart Cohen/Stone 86: (CL) Craig Lovell/Corbis 86: (BL) © Charles Gupton/Stock Boston 86: (TL) © Stuart Cohen/Image Works 86: (BR) Greg Meadors/Stock Boston 86: (TR) © Mike Timo/Stone 86: (CR) Corbis 89: (CR) Chip and Rosa Maria de la Cueva Peterson 89: (CL) PhotoDisc 90-91: (R) Brenda Joysmith Studio 90: PhotoDisc 96: (CL) © Don Fawcett/Visuals Unlimited 96: (CR) ©Breck P. Kent/Animals Animals/Earth Scenes 96: (BL) Rick Poley/Visuals Unlimited 96: (BR) Stan Elems/Visuals Unlimited 96: (BR) © Patti Murray/Animals Animals/Earth Scenes 97: (CL) © Don W. Fawcett/Visuals Unlimited 97: (B) © Patti Murray/Animals Animals/Earth Scenes 97: (CR) © Kjell B. Sandved/Visuals Unlimited 97: (BR) Zig Leszczynski/Animals Animals/Earth Scenes 98: © Dorling Kindersley 99: (C) From AN EXTRAORDINARY LIFE: THE STORY OF A MONARCH BUTTERFLY by Laurence Pringle, illustrated by Bob Marstall. Illustrations copyright ©1997 by Bob Marstall. Reprinted by permission of Orchard Books, New York. All rights reserved. 101: (C) © Dorling Kindersley109 (BL) Bettmann/Corbis-Bettmann 112: Kwanzaa by Janet Riehecky, Grolier Publishing Company-Children's Press 113: George Ancona 113: George Ancona 113: (C) Michael S. Yamashita/ Corbis 113: (B) Arthur Tilley/FPG International LLC 113: (K) Kwanzaa by Janet Riehecky, Grolier Publishing Company-Children's Press

Every effort has been made to obtain permission for all photographs found in this book and to make full acknowledgement for their use. Omissions brought to our attention will be corrected in subsequent editions.

Illustration Credits

4: Paul Sharp 5: Paul Sharp 6-7: George Thompson 8: Jay Johnson 10-11: Jane Chambless Wright 12: Michael Morris 14-15: Dee DeLoy 16-17: Eileen Mueller Neill 18-19: Cathy Ann Johnson 20-21: Darren McKee 22-23: Deborah Zemke 25: Phyllis Pollema-Cahill 26 - 27: Michael Morris 32: Lindy Burnett 34-35: Jim Ishi 36-37: Paul Sharp 40-41: Shelly Shinjo 43: Linda Pierce 44: Betsy Day 45: Tony Nuccio 46: Darren McKee 55: Linda Pierce 56-57: Elizabeth Wolf 60: Linda Pierce 66-67: Jeffrey Lindberg 68-69: Higgins Bond 70-71: Brent Cottrell 72 -73: Patti Argoff 75: Lynda Calvert-Weyant 76-77: Margeaux Lucas 80-81: Carlos Caban 82-83: Clive Scruton 88-89: Rusty Fletcher 92-93: Paul Sharp 94-95: Wayne Parmenter 96: Thea Kliros 98: Jay Johnson 98: Linda Pierce 102: Dagmar Fehlav 106: Peter Fasolino 108: Greg Harris

Acknowledgments

Credit and appreciation are due publishers and copyright owners for use of the following: 3: "A Different Beat" © 2000 Bryan Louiselle and Frog Prince Music. 5: "Windshield Wipers" from The Llama Who Had No Pajama: 100 Favorite Poems by Mary Ann Hoberman. Used by permission of Gina Maccoby Literary Agency and Harcourt, Inc. Copyright © 1974 by Mary Ann Hoberman. 11: "Phoebe" from Folk Songs of the Southern Appalachians collected by Cecil J. Sharp and edited by Maud Karpeles. © Oxford University Press 1932. Used by permission. 11: "Sing! Speak! Whisper! Shout!" © 2000 Rick Bassett. 14: "Freight Train" Words and music by E. Cotton. © Copyright 1958 by SANGA MUSIC INC. All Rights Reserved. Used by permission. 18: "Shortnin' Bread" produced and arranged by Linda Tillery. From Shakin A Tailfeather. Lead Vocal: Eric Bibb/ Supporting Vocals: The Cultural Heritage Choir. © 1997, Tuizer Music. Used by permission. 25: "To'ia Mai Te Waka" (Pull the Canoe) from Maori Games and Haka by Alan G. Armstrong. 26: "We're Making Popcorn" © 2002 Pearson Education, Inc. 31: "¡Viva el fútbol!"(I Love Soccer!) © 2000 by Rick Bassett and Gustavo Moretto. 32: "The Rain Sings a Song," from We Sing of Life by Silliman. Beacon Press, © 1960. Used by permission of the Unitarian Universalist Association. 34: "Star Light, Star Bright" © 1991 Silver Burdett Ginn. 38: "Yellow Butter" from The Llama Who Had No Pajama: 100 Favorite Poems, copyright © 1981 by Mary Ann Hoberman., reprinted by permission of Harcourt, Inc. Recorded by permission of Gina Maccoby Literary Agency. 41: "Cirmos cica" (Naughty Tabby Cat) © 2002 Pearson Education, Inc. 42: "Nampaya omame" (There Come Our Mothers) Traditional South African folk song, arranged by J. Shabalala. © 1994 Music of Windswept (ASCAP) o/b/o Gallo Music Publishers (SAMRO). All Rights administered by Windswept Pacific. All Rights Reserved. Used by Permission. WARNER BROS. PUBLICATIONS U.S. INC., Miami, FL 33014. 44: "Amefuri" (Japanese Rain Song) English version by Roberta McLaughlin and Lucille Wood. Japanese words by Kitahara Hakushu. Music by Nakayama Shinpei. © 1968 Bowmar Records Inc. © Renewed. © Assigned 1981 Belwin-Mills Publishing Corp. All Rights Reserved. Used by Permission . WARNER BROS. PUBLICATIONS U.S. INC., Miami, FL 33014. 47: "Bounce High, Bounce Low" © 1991 Silver Burdett Ginn. 48: "Chang" (Elephant) collected by Brian Burton from Milagroa Quesada at Kent State University. 51: "The Parade Came Marching" Words and music by John Forster from Family Tree by Tom Chapin. © 1988 Limousine Music Co. (ASCAP) Reprinted by permission. 55: "Yeysh Lanu Tayish" (We Have a Goat) from Roots and Branches: A Legacy of Multicultural Music for Children, by Patricia Shehan Campbell, Ellen McCullough-Brabson, and Judith Cook Tucker. Courtesy World Music Press. English words © 2002 Pearson Education, Inc. 57: "Lemonade" © 1991 Silver Burdett Ginn. 62: "Little Black Bug" Words by Margaret Wise Brown, music by Ruth Boshkoff from All Around the Buttercup. © 1984 by Schott Music Corp. All Rights Reserved. Used by permission of European American Music Distributors Corporation, Sole U.S. and Canadian agent for Schott Music Corp. 64: "B-A, Bay" from The Melody Book: 300 Selections from the World of Music by Hackett, © 1998. Reprinted by permission of Prentice-Hall, Inc., Upper Saddle River, NJ. 68: "Mammoth" from Moon Frog Text © 1992 Richards Edwards. Illustrations © 1992 Sarah Fox-Davies. Reproduced by permission of Walker Books Ltd. Published by Candlewick Press, Inc., Cambridge, MA. 70: "The Ants Go Marching" words from Sally Go Round the Sun by Edith Fowke, 1969; music from What has Become of Hinky Dinky Parlez-vous? by A. Dublin, I. Mills, J. McHugh, & I. Dash, 1924. Reprinted by permission of The Writer's Union of Canada on behalf of Edith Fowke. 72: "The Little Red Hen" © 2002 Pearson Education, Inc. 75: "I Can't Spell Hippopotamus" by J. Fred Coots. Reprinted by permission of Songwriters Guild. 77: "This Land Is Your Land" Words and music by Woody Guthrie. TRO © Copyright 1956 (Renewed) 1958 (Renewed) Ludlow Music Publishers, Inc., New York, NY Used by Permission. 78: "Ev'rybody Says" Words and music by Malvina Reynolds. Copyright © 1961 Schroder Music Co. (ASCAP); Renewed 1989. Used by permission. All rights reserved. 80: "Los Maizales (The Cornfields)," a folk song from Peru, by United States Committee for UNICEF, United Nations Children's Fund. Reprinted by permission. 82: "Scrub-a-dub" © 1996 David Eddleman. All rights reserved. 84: "Families" © 2000 James A. Forbes, Jr. 87: "Sorida" Game song from the Shona People of Zimbabwe from Let Your Voice Be Heard! by Abraham Kobina Adzenya, Dumisani Maraire and Judith Cook Tucker. Courtesy World Music Press. 88: "Banana Splits" © 2002 Pearson Education, Inc. 89: "Green, Green, Rocky" © 2002 Pearson Education, Inc. 90: "How To Be A Friend" by Pat Lowery Collins from the book You and Me, Orchard Books, 1997. Used by permission. 92: "Sailing to the Sea" Words and music by John Forster and Tom Chapin. © 1990 Limousine Music Co. & The Last Music Co. (ASCAP) Reprinted by permission. 94: "Noah's Shanty" Words and music by Malcolm Abbs, published by A & C Black Publishing Ltd. in Banana Splits. Reprinted by permission. 96: "Beach Rap" © 2002 Pearson Education, Inc. 98: "Ah! Les Jolis Papillons," (Ah! The Pretty Butterflies) from Songs For Today © 1970 Waterloo Music Co., Waterloo Canada. Reprinted with permission. English words © 2002 Pearson Education, Inc. 101: "Khorovod" from A Treasury of the World's Finest Folk Songs. Collected and arranged by Leonard Deutsch. Copyright © 1942 by Leonard Deutsch. Reprinted by permission of Crown Publishers, a division of Random House, Inc. 102: "Just Imagine" Music and lyrics by Phillip A. Parker. © 1993 Shimbaree Music (ASCAP) A division of Lyons Partnership, L.P. All Rights Reserved. Used by permission. 104: "I Know an Old Lady" Words by Rose Bonne, Music by Alan Mills. Copyright © 1952, 1954 by Peer International (Canada) Ltd. This arrangement Copyright © 2001 by Peer International (Canada) Ltd. Copyright Renewed. International Copyright Secured. All Rights Reserved. Used by permission. 106: "Hi Heidi Ho" from Lucile Panabaker's Song Book by Lucile Panabaker. Reprinted by permission of the author. 111: "The End" by A.A. Milne, copyright 1927 by E.P. Dutton, renewed © 1955 by A.A. Milne, from Now We Are Six by A.A. Milne. Used by permission of Dutton Children's Books, a division of Penguin Putnam Inc. Recorded by permission of Curtis Brown Group Ltd., on behalf of the Trustees of the Pooh Properties.

Every effort has been made to locate all copyright holders of material used in this book. If any errors or omissions have occurred, corrections will be made.

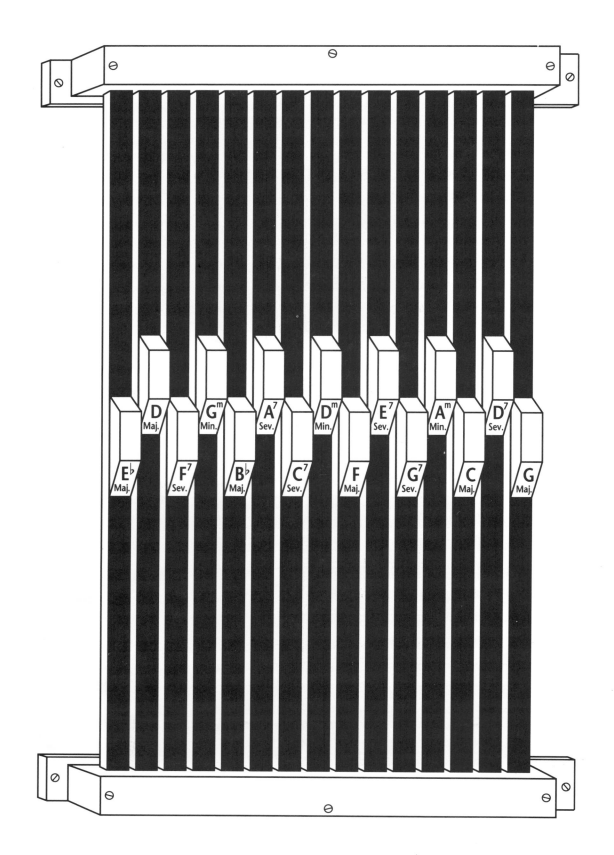